Ancient customs are still practised among the rural traditionalists. One of these is a Xhosa ritual called the *ntonjane*, which ensures the fertility of a girl when she marries. Custom demands that she is secluded in a dark hut for a period of time during which her friends go around the neighbourhood singing and dancing and collecting small gifts. These three girls (**1**) were photographed on the road to Willowvale and were part of such a colourful team of about twenty Xhosa of the Gcaleka clan.

Pondo women are easily recognized by their distinctive hairstyle, as they tend to let their hair grow much longer than the womenfolk of other Xhosa-speaking tribes. The flat, curved arrangement over this woman's ear (**2**) is plaited hair hardened with clay and dry soap, and beautified with a little black shoe polish. The strands of the back 'train' are fabric worked into the hair, and the headcloth worn as a crown points to her married status.

Girls do most of the beadwork in a family, making pieces not only for themselves but also for their boyfriends, fathers, and even their mothers at times. But often, when they really wish to look smart, they may borrow back certain pieces. Tradition and religion, however, forbid girls to wear certain men's items. Pearl buttons (**3**) are used a great deal in Xhosa beadwork.

This magnificent collection of some seventy-five pieces (**4**) belonged to Dumani Tshawe of the Kei Road area in the eastern Cape. They were so heavy that Dumani said: 'I can only wear them all for a beer drink at home. I can't walk far with them.' Tragically, not long after this photograph was taken, he lost the entire collection in a fire which razed his home.

Every piece of beadwork has a name and, though individual pieces may differ in detail, they will always be known by their common name. Photograph (**5**) shows two examples of a *lwimingwe* or 'leopard's tongue'. The red piece comes from the King William's Town area and the other from nearby Kidd's Beach. Geometric designs are conspicuous among items of Xhosa beadwork.

A man's leggings of beads on goatskin (**6**) have great religious significance, rating second in importance, first being a long multi-stranded necklace of turquoise reaching down to the waist and worn by both men and women. The wearers' ancestors 'know them' by this *danga*.

4

6

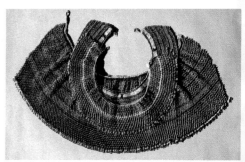

7

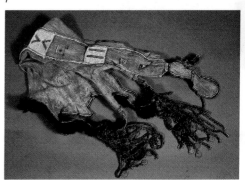

8

These collars (**7**) are among the most commonly seen neckpieces worn by senior Xhosa men, who may wear up to four of different sizes, one above the other, some with tassles reaching to the knees. Women wear similar pieces with more open patterns.

One of a Xhosa's most prized pieces is his *ngxowa yebokwe* (**8**), literally his 'bag of the goat'. In making it, the goat's body is 'extracted' through slits at the head and rear without slitting the belly area. It is worn over the left shoulder on ceremonial occasions and more for decoration than for carrying purposes. The piece shown in (**9**) is an exceptionally large example of a beaded body decoration worn by men; the central ropes rest on the wearer's shoulders, with the rectangular flaps hanging loosely at his sides.

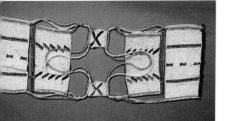

9

Country folk wear their regalia with great dignity and pride and clearl enjoy wearing it. This Xhosa girl's gay outfit (**1**) seems to symbolize t fun and happiness within her. The most important time in the life of a male Xhosa is his elevation to manhood. This lengthy ritual begins w the ceremony of circumcision, following which an initiate and his fellows undergo a three-month period of isolation during which they receive instruction in the duties of a man. Though they may not be se by womenfolk during this time, the initiates, or *kwetha*, do disguise themselves in grass outfits (**2**) and proceed around their neighbourhood giving exhibitions of their dancing. The outfits of palr leaves are heavy and painfully abrasive. But 'as men' they must end this. The skirt section alone – seen here being fitted (**3**) – weighs abc 12,5 kg.

5

6

The Pondo – though Xhosa-speaking – differ markedly in the style and colour of their dress and beadwork from the literal Xhosa tribespeople. The dress of these girls (**4**) identify them as Pondo from the Lusikisiki area of the Transkei, while the girls shown in (**5**) belong to the Xhosa tribe living around Centani. The regalia shown in (**6**) is original, but by no means traditional. This colourful old character is the praise singer – the *mbongi* – to a Bhaca chief in the Matatiele area at the foot of the Drakensberg. Acting many parts, he can recite the history, exciting adventures and deeds of his chief and his forefathers.

The Xhosa belong to a patriarchal society and a man may have any number of wives – provided he can raise the *lobolo*, or 'bride price' to recompense their fathers. Here Xhembane (**7**), who lives near Kei Road, demonstrates how a man would lead his wives in order of seniority to some ceremonial event. Draped over his shoulder is a goatskin bag like that shown in photograph (**8**) on page 3. The status of a married Xhosa woman is easily told by her headdress: the more elaborate it is, the greater her seniority.

1

This adolescent girl (**1**) wears a tight band above her breasts. This is a characteristic of the Xessibe branch of the Xhosa-speaking people wh live on the Natal border in the very northern reaches of the Transkei. Xessibe wear relatively few beads, instead placing great emphasis on armbands made of soft wire twisted around animal hair to give flexibilit Horse-tail hair is preferred to that of the ox, which has a tendency to break. Engaged Pondo girls (**2**) wear hair fringes according to the cus of *hlonipha*, or 'payment of respect', for it would be presumptious and disrespectful to 'look their boyfriends directly in the eye'. Hair worn in th manner is plaited into strands and hardened with dry soap which may mixed with clay. The strands may also be bound with cotton. The red colouring is a chemical dye mixed with oil, while the gleaming black strands are beautified with shoe polish.

Beaded headbands worn atop long tresses are the mark of a marrie Pondo woman (**3**). Such outward symbols of status are important amo traditional country folk, as they signify how people are to be treated; fo example, custom prohibits a man from engaging a married Pondo woman in conversation alone and outside of her home. Pondo enjoy sn (two of the women here wear snuff spoons, made of cattle horns, in the hair), but, unlike Xhosa men and women, they are not heavy smokers. contrast, the turban-like headdresses of other Xhosa-speaking women **& 5**) are very different. The woman pictured in (**4**) is of the actual Xhos tribe. The first joint of the little finger of her left hand is missing. It was removed, according to ancient custom, in her early years, 'to stop the

2

3

4

5

child pining away'. It is also believed, in traditionalist circles, that if it is not done the ancestors become displeased and visit sickness upon the child..

Brides are invariably conspicuous among the Xhosa-speaking peoples by their *hlonipha* procedures. Here (**5**), a senior woman of the Bomvana tribe leads a group with heads respectfully covered around the *back* of the hut to a festival at the front. The red pompoms are exclusive to the Bomvana.

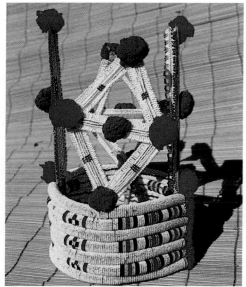

Photographs (**1**, **2**, **3 & 5**) show examples of Cele beadwork. The beaded dancing stick (**1**) indicates that this young lady is engaged to be married. The striped, celluloid bangles on her right arm are from her future husband. The Cele live in the Port Shepstone-Izingolweni area of Natal and produce some of the most attractive beadwork of all the many Zulu clans. The unusual and particularly beautiful bride's headdress shown in photograph (**3**) is from the Dweshula area near Port Shepstone. In (**5**), the eye-catching hairstyle, half dyed-red and the rest natural black, shows the young girl to be of marriageable age.

Girls of the Mabaso clan on the north side of Tugela Ferry (**4**). The large plastic beads seen around the waist of the girl nearest to the camera, and in her long string, do not, as might seem logical, necessarily mean that the piece was recently made. Although plastic beads appear to be increasing in popularity because of the cost of imported glass beads, they are also sometimes seen in fairly old pieces. Porcupine quills as worn by the girl at the back are occasionally seen among the Zulu peoples but are more common to the Swazi.

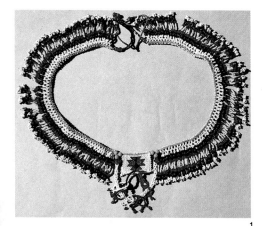

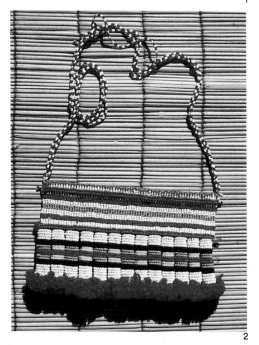

An uncommon necklace from the White Umfolozi area near Ulundi (**1**) and a further example of Cele beadwork (**2**): a popular neckpiece worn by girls. The coarse knitting wool forming the red fringe became popular with the Zulu during the Second World War when imported glass beads became difficult to obtain.

While the basic principles of Zulu dress do not vary much throughout the nation, individual characteristics often identify a specific clan. For example, these Ntombela matrons (**3**) from Mangeni are conspicuous by their striped, knitted skirts, porcupine quills (see (**4**) on previous page) and red hatband circlets.

As with the other Nguni people, a Zulu girl begins learning the art of beadworking at an early age. Mothers, older sisters and female friends are the teachers, for the country folk are sociable people and willingly give help to one another in whatever ways they are able. This scene (**4**) was photographed at Shakaland near Eshowe, where tourists can still see aspects of the old Zulu way of life.

These two girls (**5**) are from the Ngwe clan who live in the foothills of the Drakensberg, not far from Bergville. This is probably one of my most prized photographs, as their style of beadwork is seldom seen.

5

6

7

8

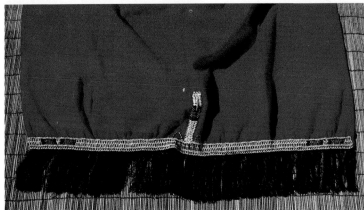

9

10

A rare set of bride's armbands (**6 & 7**) from the Msinga area near the Tugela River. The close-up shows the painstaking construction from strands of aluminium wire. The red studs enable the bands to be removed.

The Zulu are excellent potters. Of the specimens shown (**8**), that with the flange, or lip, is a carrying pot, the design preventing the contents from splashing when the pot is carried on a girl's or woman's head. The other is a drinking pot. (See my companion book, *The Zulu: their traditions and culture*, for more information on pottery.)

This unusual shoulder wrap (**9**), with its fringed end, was photographed near Port Shepstone. While the inevitable beads are conventional, the texture and colour of the cloth and the factory-made fringe show a Western influence and a deviation from tradition.

The front apron of a Zulu girl from the St Faith's area (**10**). Country folk are masters at improvization – the blue cords have been dyed with washing blue from a trader's store. The red wool of the pompoms is also from the local trader's store.

1

3

2

4

5

plugs are traditional Zulu decorations, but are not often seen
adays; certainly any as large as these (**1**), worn by a girl of the
nga area, are rare. Her face is smeared with a paste of red ochre
her hairstyle, too, is uncommon. Far more likely to be seen are
r examples of Zulu wear such as that worn by these marriageable
(**4**) at Pobana, near Eshowe, and splendid examples of Cele dress
as the apparel of this young girl (**2**), photographed at Dweshula
Port Shepstone.

diviner or *sangoma* (**3**), her elaborate headdress the obvious sign
r occupation, sitting on the skin of a freshly slaughtered white
. She had offered it up to her ancestral spirits as part of the
uation ceremony of her pupils. Before I was allowed to take any
tographs at this ceremony, the *sangoma* held a seance to ask the
roval of her spirits. Thereafter, I was requested to place a cash

donation 'for them' in the *msamo*, or sacred place, in the back of her
hut. Among the Zulu and other tribespeople, there are classifications of
sangoma, including specialists in medicine. Here, in the Msinga area,
a Thembu medicine man (**5**), with his assistant on his left, treats a
somewhat nervous patient. One of the first medications administered is
snuff in good quantity, and after this patient was given his, I had to wait
ten minutes for his sneezing to stop before taking my next picture.

While the traditional Zulu cult is ancestor worship, Christianity today
has many followers. The acceptance of Christianity does not, however,
necessarily mean the denial of all tribal custom. In the Shembe church,
for example, which has thousands of members, the importance of
traditional dress, dancing and rejoicing has not been overlooked – in
fact, as borne out by this scene (**6**), they are important parts of the
church's rites.

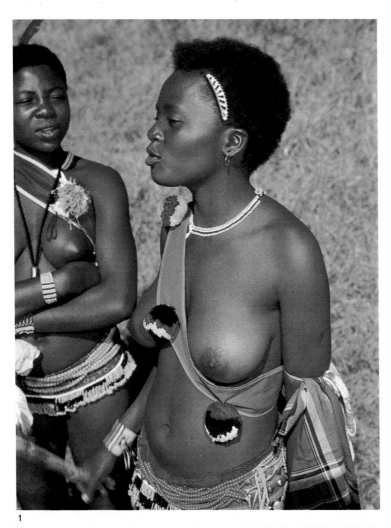

1

2

Swazi dress and regalia differ conspicuously from that of their Nguni relatives – the Xhosa, Zulu and Ndebele. Although there is less emphasis on beadwork among the Swazi, vibrant colour, gaiety and glamour are not lacking – particularly on ceremonial occasions such the *Mhlanga* or 'reed dance' (**1 & 3**), second only to the *Ncwala* (see cover caption) in national importance. The *Mhlanga* is a wonderfully colourful event held in August each year. Objects of the ceremony a to encourage friendships and, of course, it is an occasion for young women to turn out in their eye-catching regalia and to demonstrate t eligibility for marriage (only a small section of the vast number of girl who participate is shown here). But the ceremony, too, has the deep meaning of exhibiting respect for the Queen as, during the week wh the ceremony lasts, the girls walk long distances to cut and bring ba

ds for her household. Sometimes they harvest way into the dark
rs and girls are often seen carrying not only their great knives but
electric torches.

Swazi home far from city life way out under the Lebombo
untains in Kangwane (**2**). Traditionalist Swazi men are conspicuous
he style of their knobkierries as, unlike those of other Nguni people,
knob is invariably on the *side* and curved in the fashion seen here.
azi shields also differ, tending to be rounder than those of the Zulu
with longer backing sticks. Among the Swazi, colourful cotton
ts have become the accepted national dress for both men and
nen. The hair of the man is heavily plastered with blue mottled soap;
most resembles marble, and the inevitable porcupine quill is held
ily in it.

2

1 3

This picture (**1**), taken in the Bronkhorstspruit district, is exceptional in that Ndebele men in full regalia are seldom, if ever, seen today. With the man here is one of his six wives. The two long, beaded ribbons hanging from her headpiece are worn to show that she has 'a son in the mountains' – that is, in the circumcision or initiation to manhood school.

Ndebele beadwork is arguably among the finest produced by the Nguni people. Certainly they take their craft beyond just personal decoration, for, just as an artist might paint a picture for his own pleasure, so does an Ndebele often work with beads, purely for the joy of self-expression. The following pictures present the merest glimpses of their consummate skill: a bottle (**2**) which was covered and presented as a gift to a member of my family as far back as the 1940s; boys have their headpieces (**3**) made for them by their girlfriends but on special occasions they borrow from their sisters and brothers as well; an attractive piece from the Verena area (**4**) which is worn over a girl's shoulder and across her bare chest and (**6**), a variety of ceremonial dancing sticks and an axe.

4

5

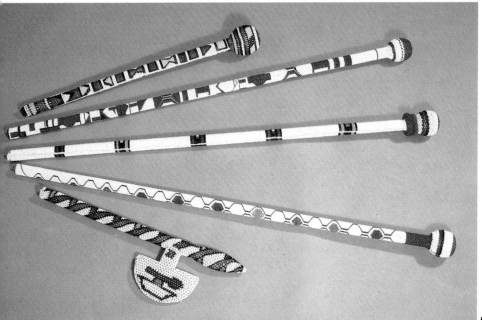

These girls (**5**) are at their 'coming out' party, a ceremony at which their emergence into marriageable status is celebrated. The weight carried and discomfort endured by a well-dressed Ndebele girl is literally quite staggering. The body hoops or bands, called *rholwani*, account for much of it. Based on the weight of the specimen shown overleaf (*photograph 3*), the girl on the right is carrying something in the vicinity of 20 kg. This, of course, includes her heavy front apron of beads on canvas, twenty-four solid brass leg bands, and a leather rear apron.

6

Some further examples of Ndebele beadwork. Gourds are used extensively by rural tribespeople, mostly for storing sour milk, but the Ndebele, who are not potters, also use them for beer. These beaded specimens (**1**) are for 'special' people.

A girl's *rholwani* (**3**) is made of grass stalks tightly bound and then covered in beads. This medium-sized specimen weighs 2,5 kg. Metal studs and coloured plastic strips are sometimes used as 'optional extras'. Another piece for a young girl is this particularly attractive necklace (**4**), while the item shown in (**5**) is worn over the back apron of a senior girl or woman on special occasions.

Great attention is given to the design and detail of a woman's aprons and here two examples are given. The first (**8**) is a five-panelled ceremonial apron, its elegance deriving from its simplicity. The second (**9**) is

2

1

3

4

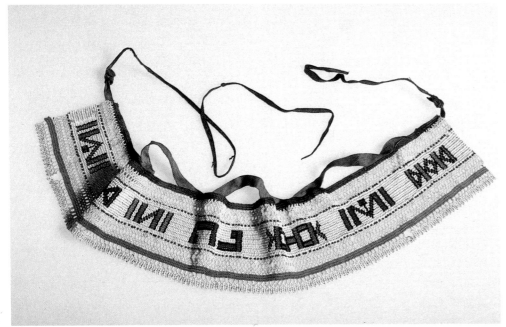

5

6

8

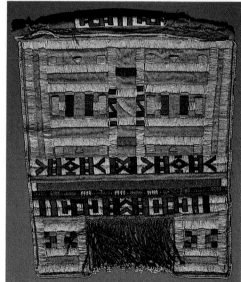

9

an apron for everyday use and is made up of beadwork on goatskin backed by heavy canvas. These canvasses often date back to the old ox-wagon days, but this specimen came from the Bronkhorstspruit area in the 1960s. While colours have tended to vary between areas and clans, darker colours – including purples and blacks – have gained in popularity in recent years.

Western influence on Ndebele dress and beadwork is inevitable; for example, the girl in (**6**) wears nylon stockings, while the cloth top of the lady in (**7**) is certainly not traditional Ndebele. Her innovative skill is to be admired, however, and she was proud of her 'modern' dress, particularly her apron, which she had made by sticking strips of coloured insulation tape over an old white plastic bag.

Contemporary images have crept into many Ndebele designs of today: aeroplanes, motor cars, and even their licence plates, are depicted in highly stylized form. An interesting example is the *telefom* held by the fellow in (**2**). As the name suggests, such elaborately beaded sticks represent the endless columns of telephone poles that run parallel to so many South African roads.

1

2

3

4

While other Nguni folk share the Ndebele love for intricate and painstakingly executed beadwork, the wonderful tradition of decorating the walls of their homes with often brilliantly coloured geometric designs is unique to these people of the Transvaal Highveld. In fact, if a single phrase could describe the Ndebele it would be difficult to find one better than 'The Artist People'. Art is in their blood and one feels they paint for the sheer joy of it. Not even the summer storms with their accompanying rains and hail, which often devastate their murals, seem to affect their enthusiasm. Sometimes Ndebele artists seem almost pleased by the opportunity to replaster their walls and to paint anew (5).

The 'canvasses' for these two works (1 & 3) were built, it seems, just to be painted on. They stood isolated without any other purpose in a village near Pretoria. It is interesting to note that the paintings are structurally almost identical, yet clever changes of colour have created different impressions. Compare, for instance, the 'steps' leading up to the 'front door' and the 'roofs' of the houses at the very top. As with beadwork, themes and images are borrowed from things outside of tradition: spirit-levels, electric lights, Western-type houses and the like. In (2 & 4) a house is again depicted, but the cool blues and whites give a quite different character. Both examples were painted on mud courtyard walls modelled especially for decoration.

5

6

7

8

On either side of its entrance, an Ndebele hut usually has a length of passage (**6**) as storage space and for children to sleep in, or even for dining in in bad weather. But walls, wherever they are, are an invitation to the artist.

Images of animals are not common in Ndebele murals, yet the skill with which the artist handled this work (**7**) at the Botshabelo Museum suggests that it would be interesting to see a lot more of her art. Almost without exception, the Ndebele artists are the womenfolk and they do not ordinarily paint on canvas or other small surfaces. 'That is the white man's way', they say.

Below is another Ndebele mural with a difference (**8**), and by the same artist, Esther Mahlangu, who has since received international recognition. In both this and the previous example, the subject matter, the precision of lines and composition, and the choice and use of colours tend to make them unique among Ndebele walls.

Traditionally, Ndebele huts are round, but in recent years increasing numbers of more Western-style, rectangular buildings are seen (**9**). Like the round, however, they are made in the centuries-old way: mud bricks, plastered with mud and cow dung.

9

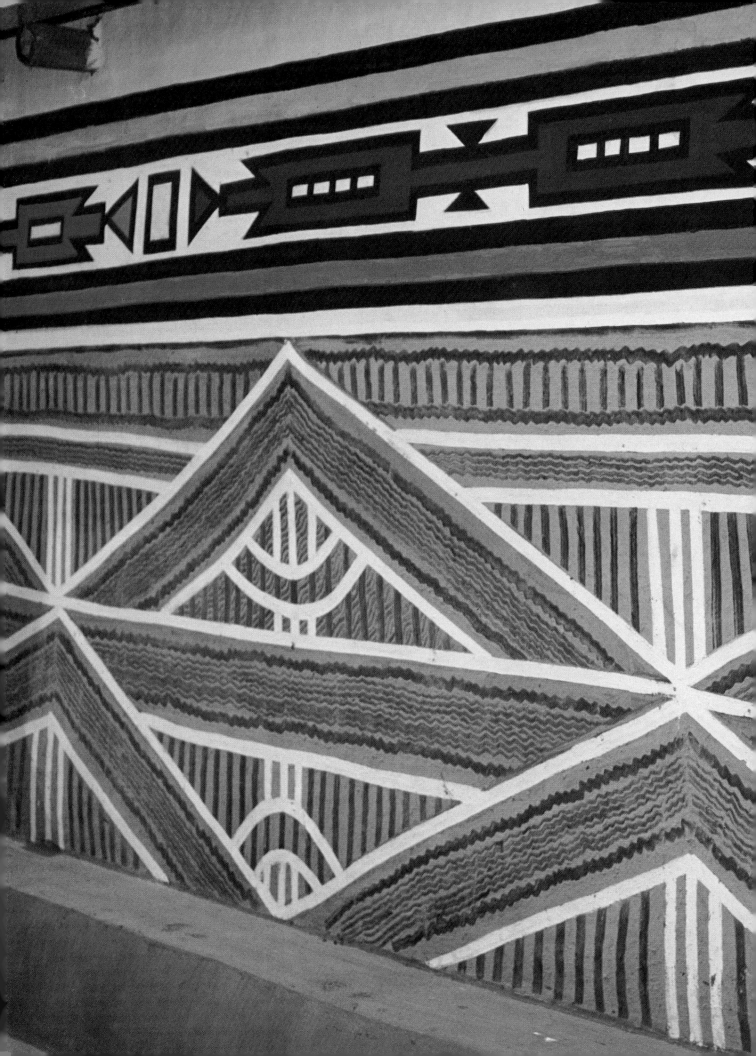

Here, again, the 'canvas' is a straight wall (**1**), and the style of decoration is a mixture of old and new. The lower section is largely finger painting with natural materials such as lime and clay and the grey has a tint of charcoal. The upper portion is modern, commercial paint applied with a brush or perhaps a bunch of fowls' wing feathers.

Photographs (**2, 3 & 4**) combined – taken from floor to thatch – cover only a small part of an interior mural about 47 metres in circumference.